TORREY PINES
Landscape and Legacy

TORREY PINES
Landscape and Legacy

Text and Photographs by Bill Evarts

Published by
Torrey Pines Association
La Jolla, California

For Dad, who shared his joy of writing books and exploring wild places.

Produced by: Cachuma Press
Editor: John Evarts
Graphic Design: Katey O'Neill
Printed in Hong Kong

Library of Congress Cataloging-in-Publication Data
Evarts, Bill, 1947–
    Torrey Pines : landscape and legacy / text and photographs by Bill Evarts. — 1st ed.
        p.   cm.
    ISBN 0-9629917-1-6
    ISBN 0-9629917-2-4 (pbk.)
    1. Torrey Pines State Reserve (Calif.) 2. Natural History—California—Torrey Pines State Reserve.
    3. Landscape—California—Torrey Pines State Reserve.
    4. Torrey Pines State Reserve (Calif.)—Pictorial works.
    I. Title.
    F868.S15E93 1994
    979.4'985—dc20   94-16320
                                                                CIP

Front Cover: Torrey pines rim a sandstone canyon in the heart of the Reserve.

Back Cover: Diverse geologic features complement the botanical wealth of Torrey Pines.

Frontispiece: The Reserve's wooded headlands rise 350 feet above Los Peñasquitos Lagoon.

CONTENTS

The Torrey pine forms the only coniferous coastal woodland in southern California.

FOREWORD

Bill Evarts came into my ranger station at the Torrey Pines Lodge in 1985. He asked me for the opportunity to explore the Reserve and to go off the main trails in order to build up a photographic record for a possible book. I agreed, not fully realizing the wonderful artwork that would come forth from that simple request.

I have had other photographers propose similar projects and ideas. But there was something about Bill and his photographs that was endearing—his sensitivity and devotion to nature, and his concern for human proportions and insights. The more I viewed his photographs, the more involved I became with the minute details and subtle interrelationships they revealed.

I grew to know this soft-voiced, bearded man over the many years we worked together to bring this project to fruition. Bill would enter the fog-enshrouded Reserve well before the gates were opened and wait for the shades of light to uncover the natural designs, often leaving well beyond sunset. In addition to spending countless hours in the field with his camera, Bill delved into the Reserve's rich cultural and natural heritage to produce this book's engaging text. His writing, like his photos, conveys a genuine affection for Torrey Pines.

When I came to Torrey Pines in 1975, the groves were lush and green and vibrant. But the statewide drought of 1986 to 1991, and a subsequent bark beetle infestation, had a severe impact on the woodlands. The beetles ravaged most of the trees in two popular groves, killing nearly 15% of the Reserve's pines. Today, I look back on the timing of Bill's arrival and his photographic efforts as incredibly fortuitous and prescient. In the seven years that he labored, he captured, and "saved" historically, some of the finest trees and scenes in the Reserve. Yet this is not a book solely of memories. Many of these "photographs" and trees are alive and with us still.

Torrey Pines was one of America's first urban preserves. It was apparent to our predecessors that this extraordinary natural confluence of earth, sky, ocean, and vegetation was worth protecting. For those of you who have "never heard of Torrey Pines," I know you are in for a pleasant surprise. And for those of you who know the Reserve well, who feel it is a close friend and spiritual confidante, I know you will rejoice and revel in the beauty that Bill uncovers and illuminates. He has caught Torrey Pines' misty somber moods and sunbathed brilliance, its finely etched microcosms and grand explosions of colorful forms and textures, all within a natural, scientific context.

This very special and private place has found its interpreter. Enjoy this revealing view of one of the best known, least known places in America.

—Robert Wohl, Supervising Ranger
Torrey Pines State Reserve

Fossil shells exposed in the Reserve's sea cliff mark the location of an earlier shore.

PREFACE

I once joined naturalist Guy Fleming for a walk at Torrey Pines, and during a pause he pulled a magnet from his pocket and told me to drag it lightly across our path. I was awestruck as tiny flecks of iron oxide jumped from the sand onto the ends of the U-shaped bar. Although I was only five at the time, I knew right away that Torrey Pines was no ordinary place.

While working on this book 40 years later, my original assessment was reaffirmed many times. Torrey Pines State Reserve is enchanting. One of my goals was to express that certain "spirit of place" so many visitors have come to love about Torrey Pines.

In searching for potential images, I followed a couple of guidelines. I excluded man-made structures from my pictures as much as possible; my primary intent was to emphasize the Reserve's natural features. I also concentrated on subjects that moved me. Most of the book's photographs were shot from the heart rather than from a prescribed list. The text evolved in a similar manner. Instead of guiding the reader through a formulaic overview, I decided to share information that had enhanced my appreciation of Torrey Pines.

There was no attempt to organize the book's photos around specific themes or correlate them directly to the text. The gallery images in particular are presented as samples of the Reserve's surprising diversity.

The success of any creative endeavor depends on the quality of support it receives. In that regard I was extremely fortunate. To all who assisted in making this book a reality, I offer my most profound thanks.

A special debt is owed Bob Wohl, Supervising Ranger at Torrey Pines. Bob shared a similar vision for this book, and without his support, the project would not have come about. I am much obliged to the entire Reserve staff for making me feel like a welcome guest. In particular, rangers Greg Hackett, Allyn Kaye, Chris Platis, and former naturalist Hank Nicol deserve recognition for their good-natured cooperation. Hank's extensive research and writing about the Reserve also made my job easier.

I'm grateful to the Torrey Pines Association for so generously taking on this project. I wish to thank the members of the Association's book committee who volunteered their valuable time to consult on the book's content and style. I'm especially indebted to two-term committee chairman John Shelton, who helped shepherd this project through its lengthy evolution.

I greatly appreciate the efforts of those technical reviewers who kindly brought their expertise and knowledge to bear on the manuscript. The following individuals deserve special acknowledgment for their critiques: Bob Haller, University of California, Santa Barbara; Geoff Levin, (formerly) San Diego Museum of Natural History; Thomas Oberbauer, County of San Diego; and Bill Tippets, (formerly) California Department of Parks and Recreation. Other experts who commented on sections of the text include Pat Abbott, San Diego State University; Dan Cayan and Doug Inman, Scripps Institution of Oceanography; Mike Wells, California Department of Parks and Recreation; and Steve Veirs and William Halvorson, National Park Service.

Special thanks are also due John Evarts of Cachuma Press who went the extra mile in all phases of the book's editing, design, and production.

The City of San Diego first set aside land for a park at Torrey Pines in 1899.

ONE

SPARING THIS TREE

Why should not San Diego, within whose corporate limits this straggling remnant of a past age finds a last lingering resting place, secure from threatened extermination this remarkable and unique Pacific Coast production?

—C. C. Parry, 1883

Several months before the territory of California achieved full statehood, Charles Christopher Parry rode north along the coast from the pueblo of San Diego. He had been sent by his employer to search for a sea-bluff deposit of coal, but the young naturalist also hoped to investigate reports of some unusual conifers. While Parry located only traces of coal, he did make an important botanical find. Little did he know that his discovery would later become the focal point of a historic conservation battle. The year was 1850.

A Find for Science

Parry, a medical doctor with a strong interest in botany, first arrived in San Diego in July 1849. At age 26 and already a veteran of two government expeditions in the Midwest, he had been appointed official botanist of the U.S.-Mexican Boundary Survey. Following the Mexican-American War (1846-48), the survey was commissioned to map and document the newly revised border between the U.S. and Mexico. Parry was first sent to the Yuma region of Arizona, and after completing his assignment he returned to San Diego and worked for the commander of the survey's military escort.

Entomologist John Le Conte, who was then visiting the area, had asked Parry about some peculiar pines growing above the mouth of Soledad Valley (now called Sorrento Valley).

Piqued by Le Conte's query, Parry garnered an assignment to check out rumored coal deposits in the sea cliffs adjacent to Soledad. Upon reaching the site by way of the beach, Parry ascended the bluffs in order to measure and sketch the exposed strata. He reported "it was necessary to follow up some of the sharp ravines that here debouch on the

The Torrey pine was named by physician-naturalist Charles Parry, who noted its "distorted branches loaded down with ponderous cones."

ocean beach, and here (possibly to the neglect of strict geological duties) my attention was taken up by this singular and unique maritime pine, which, with its strong clusters of terminal leaves and its distorted branches loaded down with ponderous cones, was within easy reach of botanical clutch."

Anticipating that the pine was unknown to science, Parry sent sample material for verification to his mentor, eminent American botanist John Torrey. In writing Torrey he included a generous request: "I here found a new species of pine growing in sheltered places about the bluff. Its characters are so unique I am in hopes it may be nondescript. . . . I wish it with your permission to bear the name *Pinus torreyana*." The tree proved to be both a new species and an exceedingly rare pine. At that time, it was only known to grow on sandstone bluffs along a narrow, five-mile strip of coast on the northern outskirts of San Diego.

Although Charles Parry received credit for recognizing the species as new, he obviously wasn't the first to become aware of the trees. Native Americans living in the San Diego region were familiar with the pines that grew near Soledad Valley. Delphina Cuero, a Kumeyaay Indian who grew up along the coast, relates in her autobiography that her group "used to gather pine nuts right near the ocean near San Diego beyond La Jolla" as recently as the early 1900s. Following the establishment of a mission in San Diego in 1769 by the Spanish, the region became known as *Soledad*, and the trees were later called Soledad pines. Historians believe that European mariners who began charting the California coast in the sixteenth century used the distinctive pine-topped sea cliffs, called *Punta de los Arboles* (Point of Trees) as a navigational aid. The pines continued to be used as a sailors' landmark well into the nineteenth century, as confirmed by the *Coast Pilot*, a volume of coastal sailing directions. The journal's 1889 edition labeled the highest prominence "Pine Hill," and added: "As this is the only pine-covered hillock for miles along this coastline it is an important landmark to vessels that are running close along shore in foggy weather."

Parry identified hundreds of new plants in California and the West during his distinguished career, but probably few species were as important to him as the Torrey pine. Not surprisingly, he was the first to champion the rare tree and call for its preservation. Thirty years after he first encountered the species, he returned to the seaside groves. Parry soon concluded that the unique trees deserved protection. In 1883 he wrote an account of his discovery for the fledgling San Diego Society of Natural History, and in prose as contorted as the scrappy trees he wished to save he also delivered a challenge:

Here, seeking shelter from the fervid rays of a February sun under the scant shade of this decrepid forest monarch, listening to the sullen dash of the Pacific waves against the bold shores, among other . . . thoughts suggested by the inspiring scene . . . one [thought] floats uppermost like drifting seaweed and finds a fitting expression here. Why should not San Diego, within whose corporate limits this straggling remnant of a past age finds a last lingering resting place, secure from threatened extermination this remarkable and

Charles Parry's detailed description of the sea bluffs at Torrey Pines was printed in the Boundary Survey's final report published in 1859.

unique Pacific Coast production so singularly confined within its boundaries, dedicating this spot of ground . . . forever to the cause of scientific instruction and recreation? Where wiser generations than ours may sit beneath its ampler shade and listening to the same musical waves thank us for 'sparing this tree?' And finally why is not the San Diego Society of Natural History the suitable body to recommend such action?

In urging local authorities to safeguard the pines for posterity, Parry became an early advocate of the uniquely American idea that began budding during the late nineteenth century: protection of rare or scenic natural areas for the enjoyment of future generations. His proposal to establish a natural reserve within the boundaries of a city was probably the first of its kind in the West. At that time, America's preservation movement was still in its infancy and would not gain countrywide momentum until 1889, when John Muir led the campaign to create a national park around California's Yosemite Valley.

A Free and Public Park

The San Diego Society of Natural History responded to Parry's appeal by appointing a committee to lobby for the trees' protection. In 1885 San Diego officials posted signs that ordered a $100 reward "for the detection and conviction of any person guilty of removing, cutting, or otherwise destroying any of the Torrey Pines now growing in Soledad and vicinity." Unfortunately, the tough-worded signs failed to deter wood gatherers. J. G. Lemmon, who was hired by the newly formed California State Board of Forestry to study the state's pine trees in 1887-88, reported evidence of tree cutting and seedling removal among the Torrey pines. He felt the trees could be better protected under state auspices. Lemmon predicted that "with the influx of immigration this lovely seaside area is destined to receive a large population, and then these trees will be menaced with extermination at the hands of men."

Soon after San Diego had taken the first measures to protect the seaside pines, a surprising find was made on Santa Rosa Island, 175 miles northwest of the city. In 1888

Naturalists have long been aware of the rich plant communities at Torrey Pines. Prickly pear, yarrow, and buckwheat flourish on the Reserve's headlands.

botanist T. S. Brandegee reported small groves of Torrey pine on the island, which lies about 27 miles southwest of Santa Barbara. The island trees raised perplexing questions about the species' discontinuous range, but did little to diminish the fact that the pine was exceptionally rare. No other native Torrey pine enclaves have ever been discovered.

Despite San Diego's growing awareness of this botanical treasure, degradation of the Torrey pine habitat continued. The city leased its undeveloped holdings for sheep and cattle grazing in 1890, including lands where the pines were located. Cattlemen cut and burned the chaparral, probably along with some pines, to improve forage for their livestock. Botanist Belle Angier surveyed the area in 1895 and warned of the potential demise of the trees. At her urging, city father George Marston, naturalist Daniel Cleveland, and members of the San Diego Society of Natural History intensified their pressure on the city council. Finally, on August 8, 1899, the city formally set aside 369 acres as a "free and public park" and declared "that there is growing upon said land certain rare and valuable trees of the variety known as *Pinus torreyana*, and that it is the wish and desire of the said City of San Diego to preserve said trees." This local civic action preceded by four years the opening of the state's first park for a far more famous native tree, the towering coast redwood of northern California.

The creation of what became known as Torrey Pines Park was a good initial step, but it contained no provisions for actually protecting the endangered groves. Furthermore, a number of adjacent parcels with Torrey pines that the city had sold 30 years earlier were slated for subdivision. At the behest of George Marston, San Diego's well-known philanthropist Miss Ellen Browning Scripps came to the rescue. By 1912 she had purchased the private lots and generously held them in trust for the people of San Diego.

Although the heart of the area was now spared from development, woodcutting remained a persistent threat. Another botanical survey was conducted by horticulturist and naturalist Guy L. Fleming in 1916 on behalf of the San Diego Floral Association and Society of Natural History. His findings confirmed that the pines were still being chopped up for firewood by campers and picnickers, and he estimated there were only about 200 trees left. Fleming suggested that the Torrey Pines area be made a national park. His disturbing report led to renewed interest in saving the species and the surrounding environment. In 1921 Miss Scripps hired Fleming as custodian for her holdings as well as the city's. Parry's wish now seemed fulfilled.

Guarding and Preserving

With the Park consolidated, Ellen Scripps financed the construction of a Southwest-style adobe lodge as a gift to the city. For many years it housed a popular roadside restaurant, and today the building contains

An inviting path winds through Parry Grove, one of four groves at the Reserve. Mojave yucca exemplifies the botanical diversity of this coastal woodland.

a visitors' center and rangers' offices. Miss Scripps also retained prominent Los Angeles landscape architect Ralph D. Cornell to develop a management plan for the Park. Cornell was quick to appreciate the area's unique setting and its rich assemblage of species. The Park's aesthetic aspects, however, impressed him most. In his 1922 report, he enthused: "In a small way such a place as Torrey Pines ranks among the natural phenomena and should hold its small, though proud place among our national monuments

While calling for modest reforestation, landscape architect Ralph Cornell felt that picturesque slopes "should not be concealed" by excessive planting.

to nature's ability as a temperamental artist who now and then exceeds even her own hopes in the creation of something unusually attractive."

Fearful that Torrey Pines Park might become a botanic garden, Cornell opposed any major alteration of the landscape or introduction of plants and features "foreign to the spirit and feeling" of the area. Although he believed that any development should be undertaken "thoughtfully and restrainedly," Cornell was not opposed to some embellishment of the natural setting. He favored decorative planting of native wildflowers and tolerated the presence of nonnative species as long as they were attractive and doing well.

Cornell observed a lack of young trees within the Park and recommended that Torrey pine seedlings be set out as future replacements for the older specimens. Consistent with his philosophy, he emphasized an artistic approach to the tree planting, urging that the new pines "be irregularly and thinly spotted, placed in crevices, on ledges and pinnacles where they can be so established, and generally handled in thoughtful consideration for their natural appearance. Do not heavily clothe the slopes; retain the bare, open spaces; remember, that to be enjoyed, both trees and views must be visible." How much of his plan was implemented is unknown, but comparison of today's landscape with historic photos suggests that a number of pines were planted in the area of the lodge.

Bowing to renewed pressure from conservationists, the city transferred more of its property to the Park in 1924. The additional land included sea cliffs, canyons, mesas, a salt marsh, and several miles of beach frontage, increasing the Park to nearly 1,000 acres. Ellen Scripps responded by adding a codicil to her will to transfer her property at Torrey Pines to the city upon her death. It contained the reminder that "permanent preservation of those rare trees and securing in perpetuity the scenic beauty of that region is vital." She also authorized the construction of an on-site residence for Guy Fleming, which was completed in 1927.

Fleming was given lifelong tenure to the house and managed the Park until Ellen Scripps' death in 1932. The following year he went to work for the State Division of Parks as Southern District Superintendent while keeping his residential office at Torrey Pines. His son, John Fleming, served part-time as the Park's patrolman and maintenance man until the Scripps property was finally transferred to the city. Although management of Torrey Pines was now the city's responsibility, the Fleming family voluntarily helped maintain and protect the Park until they moved to nearby La Jolla in 1958.

The first major threat to the Park arose in 1929 when commercial interests urged building a high-speed highway through Torrey Pines. The proposed road was designed to bypass a narrow, winding grade (now used only for access to the lodge), which created a bottleneck on the major thoroughfare between San Diego and Los Angeles. One scheme called for blasting away 1,700 feet of sea cliff for a straight, more gradual right-of-way from the beach to the mesa top. Debris from cutting in the new alignment was to be dumped onto the public beach. One scenic canyon was to be crossed on an embankment of fill and another

spanned by a bridge.

Opposition to this proposal was led by The League to Save Torrey Pines Park. Its members felt the best solution was to build a new road to the east via Sorrento Valley, skirting Torrey Pines altogether. In a brochure that addressed numerous reasons for preventing the road, the League answered its own

Cleveland sage grows at the Reserve and is named for Daniel Cleveland, a naturalist and early sponsor of Torrey Pines' protection.

rhetorical question, "Is the danger to the Park very pressing?" with the following blast: "So pressing that only an immediate and emphatic expression of public disapprobation . . . can save this heritage of the people from a defilement which will bring upon its perpetrators the condemnation of generations yet unborn." A compromise was reached in 1930, and a grade (old Highway 101, now North Torrey Pines Road) was cut through the eastern part of the Park's uplands instead of along the cliffs. The region's modern freeway (Interstate 5) was eventually built east of Torrey Pines, following the route favored by the League 40 years earlier.

Concern over the despoliation of Torrey Pines surfaced again during the 1940s. The negative impact that a relatively small number of visitors inflicted upon the Park's sensitive habitat was alarming. People still foraged for firewood among the groves. Hikers climbed the high points, eroding sandy soils and exposing vulnerable pine roots. Careless tourists left a growing accumulation of trash and litter. Many residents felt that the city had been lax in its administration of the Park.

After Guy Fleming published an article about Torrey Pines in *Western Woman* magazine in 1942, he confided to the director of the National Park Service that his story was "written with the hope that it would stimulate a more aggressive guardianship of these unique trees." Fellows of the San Diego Society of Natural History urged that the parcels donated by Ellen Scripps be dedicated as a wildlife

Acquisition of the wetlands habitat adjacent to Torrey Pines began in 1924. Los Peñasquitos Lagoon provides sanctuary for numerous waterfowl such as mallards.

area and natural preserve, noting that "such examples of Nature's handiwork are rare, and, unfortunately for posterity, are fast disappearing through man's carelessness." Trustees of the Ellen Browning Scripps Foundation, established several years after her death, were more blunt in their assessment: "The Park has been neglected since the city received this remarkable gift of Torrey Pines Point from Miss Scripps, and no provision has been made for guarding and preserving this precious heritage." In 1948 Fleming retired from his state position in order to direct his energies toward finding public or private support for the Park.

Ralph Cornell was again hired by the Foundation to draw up new management guidelines. He now believed the main problem was accommodating increased public use, and urged the creation of a detailed master plan for trails, picnic areas, and related recreational facilities. He also proposed that the northern portion of the Park be designated as a strict wilderness conservation area. Cornell called for better maintenance and policing at Torrey Pines. Perhaps most importantly, he advocated creating a private organization that could assist in establishing Park policies, raise funds for Park needs, and help educate the public about sensitive resources at Torrey Pines.

Following Cornell's suggestion, the Foundation recommended the formation of a cooperating association. To that end the Torrey Pines Association was established in 1950 with Guy Fleming as its first president. One of the Association's early goals was to promote the transfer of Torrey Pines Park from the city to California's Division of Beaches and Parks (now the Department of Parks and Recreation). In a special election in 1956 San Diegans approved conveying the Park to the state, a process that was completed by 1959. The official designation was changed to Torrey Pines State Reserve.

During the late 1960s, the Association helped spearhead the biggest event in the Reserve's recent history. Prime stands of privately held Torrey pines on the north side of the Reserve's Los Peñasquitos Lagoon were threatened by development. Mounting a grass-roots fundraising effort that received national attention, local citizens augmented state moneys, contributing nearly half the funds needed to purchase the endangered pine habitat. Annexation of the area, known as the Torrey Pines Extension, began in 1970 and enlarged the Reserve by nearly 200 acres. In addition to its robust pine specimens and delicate geologic features, the Extension supports several plant species not found in the main Reserve.

Today, the state's combined beach, lagoon, and upland units comprise approximately 1,750 acres and are informally referred to as "Torrey Pines." Two restricted and sensitive areas within the Reserve have also been designated: Ellen B. Scripps Natural Preserve and Los Peñasquitos Marsh Natural Preserve. The beach area is classified as a State Beach.

Sparked by Parry's foresight, successive generations have fought vigorously to save the Torrey pine and the unique environment it inhabits. Given the fact that the tree has no commercial value and occupies some of southern California's most coveted coastal real estate, it is all the more remarkable that this effort culminated in a State Reserve. A profound debt of gratitude is owed to all those who have assisted in "sparing this tree."

For more than a century the Torrey pine has had its champions. It has become a source of civic pride and a symbol of hope for those working to preserve other rare and endangered species.

*T*he predominant plant community on the Torrey Pines headlands is chaparral, which some botanists distinguish as southern maritime chaparral. Although similar to the widespread chaparral communities of California's foothills, the coastal version is distinct. Of the roughly six remaining stands of southern maritime chaparral in San Diego County, the Reserve's assemblage is special because it includes the Torrey pine and a number of other rare species.

*T*he coast at Torrey Pines has undergone many changes. The 45-million-year-old sandstone layers at the north end of the cliffs record a period when the shore migrated back and forth in response to fluctuating sea level and intermittent uplift. Evidence of at least six distinct shorelines from the past 500,000 years is preserved on the headlands in the form of shore deposits, wave-cut benches, and coastal sand dunes.

The alchemy of evening is perhaps best appreciated from the Reserve's cliff-top trails and overlooks. Once the sun has set, only essential ingredients remain. Captured in this time exposure are rocks in the sand, swirling surf, and reflections of the departing light.

*T*he ebb and flow of nature is manifested in countless cycles and patterns. At the onset of summer, canchalagua blooms amidst drying grasses in the Reserve's open areas. Brisk onshore breezes course over the headlands each day during this time of year.

Coastal agave is extremely rare in southern California, and this patch at Torrey Pines may represent the northernmost edge of the species' natural range. It grows most abundantly in Baja California's central desert plains and northwest coast. This unique combination of pine needles and desert succulents speaks volumes about the Reserve's surprising assemblage of plants.

Torrey Pines' beach cobbles have survived a long history of abrasion. Originally transported to the coast by rivers, the hard stones have been pummeled by streams and waves through countless cycles of erosion. Each summer gentle waves bury them beneath loads of sand, but by winter, strong surf strips the sand away again. Freshly exhumed cobbles are rolled back and forth across the beach by a ceaseless parade of waves.

The Reserve's friable sandstone often proves to be treacherous footing for a Torrey pine. Some trees tilt, or almost tip over, when their anchoring roots become exposed and lose their purchase in the soft sandstone. The pines often compensate by developing asymmetrical growth.

Slowly undercut by the rasping action of waves, the cliff face collapses and buries the beach with great chunks of sandstone. Weathering and abrasion round the edges of these blocks, while further wave action removes newly released grains of sand. By advancing against the cliff, the waves continue their incremental cutting of a new bench at the level of the current beach.

17

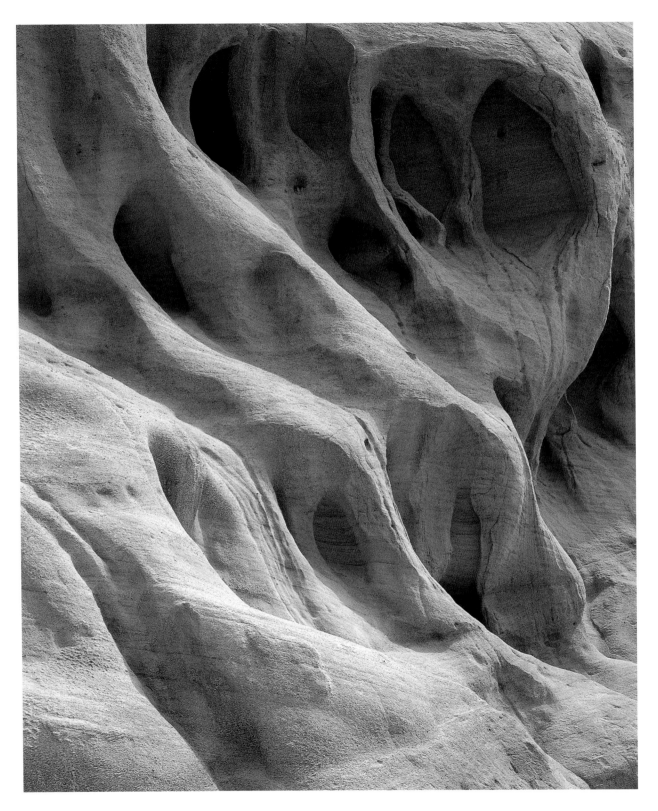

Sometimes called "wind caves," these sinuous cavities are not carved by the wind but are instead the product of chemical weathering. Rainwater seeps into the sandstone and slowly dissolves the natural cement that holds the rock's grains together. Various factors, such as the degree of water penetration and moisture retention, contribute to the uneven disintegration of the sandstone. Wind helps remove the loosened grains and keep the hollows tidy.

Mojave yucca is dependent on a single species of Tegeticula *moth for pollination. The female moth collects pollen from one flower, places it on the stigma of another, and deposits her eggs in that flower's ovary. The moth larvae eat a small percentage of the developing yucca seeds before exiting the plant. This mutually beneficial relationship ensures efficient pollination and provides a source of food for the moth's offspring.*

Two drought-adapted plant communities, coastal sage scrub and chaparral, grow right to the water-logged margin of Los Peñasquitos Lagoon. California sagebrush, bladderpod, bush sunflower, lemonadeberry, coast cholla, and prickly pear descend the slopes and abruptly give way to carpets of pickleweed at the edge of the salt marsh.

In an effort to gain support for Torrey Pines in the 1940s, naturalist Guy Fleming encouraged visitors to "discover for yourself the spell that is cast upon those who visit this last resting place of a vanishing forest. Take home with you the vision of beauty unfolded."

Ancestors of the Torrey pine may have originated in west-central Mexico some 45 million years ago.

A Spirit Captured

For more than a century, the Torrey pine has been recognized as America's rarest pine. Native stands are found in only two locales, both in southern California: one is near the northern edge of San Diego and the other on Santa Rosa Island southwest of Santa Barbara. Together at the two sites there are about 10,000 trees; combined, they occupy less than 1,000 acres. Only the Dalat pine, discovered in Vietnam in 1960, and several other pines in Mexico may be more limited in range and number. In addition to being one of the nation's rarest trees, the Torrey pine is also among the most vulnerable. Recent studies portray it as a species with an intriguing history but an uncertain future.

Straggling Remnants

Much of our knowledge about the Torrey pine's past is based on conjecture, but scientists believe they can trace its origins to west-central Mexico. Beginning about 45 million years ago, the climates of the Southwest and northern Mexico began a drying trend that led to significant diversification among North American pines. Prior to that time, the conifers growing in Mexico's interior uplands were adapted to a temperate climate. In response to the long cycles of drought, a number of species migrated south where a more tropical climate

Of the Torrey pine, Charles Parry wrote that "this singular species may be seen to best advantage clinging to the face of crumbling yellow sandstone."

Coulter pine and gray pine are the Torrey pine's closest relatives, and together the three are known as the big-coned pines. Botanists theorize that the forerunners of these pines arrived in southern California at the same time. Starting about 25 million years ago, the northwest coast of Mexico began to break away from the mainland. What was to become present-day Baja California and much of western California started drifting northward along a complex zone of faults where two of the earth's tectonic plates abut. This displacement could have transported the big-coned species and other flora from coastal Mexico to southern California. The three pines subsequently exploited separate niches and differentiated into a maritime (Torrey) and two inland (Coulter and gray) species.

Despite its enigmatic past, scientists have reason to believe that the Torrey pine has existed for a long time. Botanists cite the slow evolution of pines in general, and the many differences between the Torrey pine and its big-coned relatives in particular, as evidence that *Pinus torreyana* is an old species.

It is difficult to know how widespread the Torrey pine may have been, but most researchers believe the species was always restricted to a temperate coastal strip. Maritime conditions with moderate temperatures, high humidity, and abundant fog probably contributed to its survival, especially during extended dry periods. Since no Torrey pine fossils have been discovered, direct evidence of its historic range is lacking. The absence of fossils may be explained by the species' occupation of exposed, erodible sites, which were not conducive to fossil preservation. It is also possible that Torrey pine populations were always small and their distribution limited.

Why the pines occur where they do today is an

offered greater summertime moisture; they also moved upward in elevation to less arid mountainous areas. Another group of pines, which probably included the ancestors of the Torrey pine, migrated west to the coast where conditions were more moderate.

unsolved mystery. It has been suggested, for example, that the Reserve is foggier and cooler than adjacent coastal areas and is therefore more favorable for the Torrey pine. This hypothesis, however, has not been investigated by scientists. Another factor that may affect the pine's current distribution is soil type. At the Reserve, a majority of the trees grow in coarse, sandy soil derived from ancient shore and dune deposits. The Torrey pines on Santa Rosa Island are also found on porous, somewhat sandy soil.

A Tale of Two Pines

The wide separation between the Torrey pine's two isolated populations has long puzzled scientists. Detailed studies have shown that the two groups are distinct from each other. Differences in cone and seed morphology, needle color, and growth forms are great enough that some botanists consider the Santa Rosa Island pine to be a separate subspecies, *Pinus torreyana insularis*. Slight genetic differences between the mainland and island trees have also been detected.

Several hypotheses have been put forth to explain why the only sites supporting native groves of Torrey pine are so far apart. Most researchers are not yet convinced by any one explanation, but consider several as plausible. One of the theories relies on geological evidence that links at least two of the Channel Islands to the San Diego region. According to some geologists, the landmass that became the basis of the northern Channel Islands split off from the San Diego mainland 10 to 20 million years ago and was moved northward along offshore faults. If Torrey pines were growing along the San Diego coast at that time, such tectonic movement could account for the species' presence

on Santa Rosa Island. Some botanists discount this idea, noting that greater genetic differences than currently exist between the two groups would have evolved over such a long period of separation.

Another theory is that the Santa Rosa Island population is older than the one at the Reserve. Based on studies of the age and distribution of other island flora, it suggests that the Torrey pine could have arrived on the offshore archipelago from a mainland source as early as three million years ago. During the Ice Age, which began about two million years ago, the Torrey pine may have been eradicated from the mainland, but survived on the offshore islands where conditions were probably more moderate. Sea levels fluctuated during the Ice Age, falling when water was locked up in the ice sheets, and rising when they melted. Within the last one million years, when a drop in sea level may have occurred during a cool, moist stage, the pines could have recolonized the mainland. This sequence of events provides enough time for the development of small genetic differences between island and coastal populations. The species' arrival at the Reserve, whether from an island or other mainland site, must have occurred within the last 500,000 years, since Torrey Pines was below sea level prior to that time.

A third hypothesis suggests that the island trees became established more recently by seed from a mainland Torrey pine grove. It is unlikely, however, that seed from a San Diego group could have drifted north to Santa Rosa Island because the prevailing coastal current flows to the south. Instead, the seed source was probably a grove that once existed on the coast near the islands. The most recent lowering of sea level due to Ice Age glacial advances occurred about 18,000 years ago, when only four miles separated the offshore landmass from the mainland. At that time, seeds could have traveled across the narrow strait in floating pine cones or perhaps have been carried by birds. Pine seeds could also have been transported to the island within the last 10,000 years by Native Americans.

Survival on the Sea Cliffs

When compared to its more stately cousins, such as sugar or ponderosa pines, the Torrey pine looks like the proverbial poor relation. Confined to nutrient-poor sandstone soils and frayed by salty coastal breezes, this eccentric-looking tree clings singly to eroding ridges or forms small, unpretentious groves. In his *Silva of California* (1910), Willis Jepson belittled the species: "The trees themselves are . . . disappointing. They are insignificant in stature and habit, and notwithstanding that they are the only trees

Limited to a narrow maritime range, coastal scrub oak forms thickets on the Reserve's windswept headlands.

where they grow they dominate the landscape so little as scarcely to be noticed except by the traveller acquainted with the peculiarities which give them a singular interest." Of course those very "peculiarities" have helped endear the pine to many generations of conservationists, artists, visitors, and local citizens.

The Torrey pine normally grows to about 35 feet; in protected locations it may reach 70 feet or more. Its trunk can exceed three feet in diameter, but such thickness is unusual because the tree often divides into multiple trunks near its base. The tree's ponderous limbs sweep outward and upward, forming broad crowns with a candelabra-like appearance. Mature specimens are often broader than they are tall. On more exposed bluffs and headlands, the pine may be recumbent or asymmetrical in profile.

Sculpted by the elements and often displaying distorted limbs and angular branches, many of these photogenic trees look ancient. Their weathered appearance is deceptive: the Torrey pine is relatively short-lived, with an average life span of only 125 years. By comparison, western bristlecone and foxtail pines may live several thousand years. The longest-lived tree in Torrey Pines State Reserve was about 200 years old. The Santa Rosa Island groves contain several 250-year-old specimens.

The Torrey pine is an exceptionally fast grower when situated in a favorable location. At the Reserve, some seaward trees may spend their lives sprawling near the ground, but protected individuals can add three or more feet in a season. This characteristic makes the Torrey pine a popular ornamental where a rapid-growing landscape tree is desired. The world's largest Torrey pine is located in the coastal community of Carpinteria. The tree was transplanted as a seedling from Santa Rosa Island in 1888, the same year the island groves were discovered. In its centennial year it measured 128 feet high, with a crown spread of 121 feet and a trunk circumference of nearly 20 feet.

Although the Torrey pine and its ancestors probably migrated to escape dry climates, the species exhibits a variety of attributes that help it survive in an environment where rainfall is minimal. Its root system, for example, is extensive and deep. A six-inch seedling often has a tap root several feet long. A mature tree can wedge its tap root 25 feet into the sandstone bluffs to search out water and nutrients. Its shallow lateral roots may extend more than 200 feet in order to capture surface moisture. In some situations the pine's penetrating roots become a liability. They often enlarge fractures in the sandstone, especially along cliff faces; this induces erosion near the pine's footing and makes the tree more vulnerable to high winds that can topple it.

The Torrey pine's long needles, which are typically bundled five to a sheath, are tough enough to withstand frequent thrashing by maritime winds. Like the leaves of many plants in arid regions, they are covered by a thick waxy coating that reduces water loss. Their low surface area retards transpiration and their light gray-green color helps reflect intense sunlight. Averaging nine inches in length, the coarse needles are efficient at collecting droplets of fog, which then drip to the ground and dampen the soil directly beneath the tree. Studies are currently underway at the Reserve to measure the amount of fog drip and evaluate its contribution to the survival of the Torrey pine.

Torrey pine cones are four to six inches long and harbor about 100 seeds each. Individual trees support both male and female cones. The female cone buds, which number about 100 per tree per season, grow most abundantly on the higher branches; they initially resemble

The Torrey pine is unusual because it sometimes grows female conelets and pollen-producing male cones on the same branch.

miniature red cones. The male cones develop mostly on the lower limbs and look similar to willow catkins. In February the male cones produce clouds of yellow pollen that dust the trees and surrounding vegetation at the slightest breeze. The small, red, female conelets secrete a sticky substance that traps the airborne pollen grains. The conelets continue to grow, although it may take a year or more for the captured pollen to penetrate the ovary and complete fertilization. The male cones dry up and drop off the tree by summer.

In nearly every other pine species, the cone-growing cycle is completed within two years. Torrey pine cones, however, require nearly three years to reach maturity, and the tightly closed cones weigh up to a pound or more. On average, only about 10 of the initial 100 cone buds will eventually mature into full-grown, seed-bearing cones, but

---

Sea dahlias are rare in southern California, but flourish throughout the Reserve, especially under the pines.

this fluctuates greatly from one year to the next. In the fall the three-year-old cones slowly unseal and begin to release their precious cargo. The large and hard-shelled pine seeds plummet directly to the ground because their short wings are inadequate for wind-aided dispersal.

Even though hundreds of seeds may fall from a tree in a single season, less than a dozen are likely to reach the seedling stage. Most won't penetrate the layer of organic duff built up beneath the parent tree and come in contact with bare soil, a necessity for successful germination.

While rodents and birds eat the majority of seeds, industrious scrub jays may unwittingly assist in the tree's propagation. Scrub jays have been observed hoarding excess Torrey pine seeds by burying them for later consumption. Since the jays often fail to retrieve all of their stash, some of the interred seeds may later sprout and produce seedlings. Researchers are studying scrub jay behavior at the Reserve to determine whether these acquisitive birds are significant "planters" of the Torrey pine.

With sufficient rainfall, Torrey pine seeds germinate after lying dormant for the winter. The seedlings emerge in early spring. This is a precarious stage in the life of a Torrey pine. Damping-off fungus, hungry rabbits, and summer heat exact high rates of mortality. Over the span of a century, a healthy tree may give rise to nearly a thousand seedlings, yet only one of these is likely to survive to replace the parent when it falls.

Of Closed Cones and Wildfire

Botanists surmise that many conifers now growing in California, including the Torrey pine, were exposed to the regular occurrence of wildfires during their lengthy evolution. In some species, this may have led to the development of specialized cones that remain tightly closed long after their seeds are fully mature—a characteristic called serotiny. During a fire, serotinous cones normally protect their seeds, yet it is the fire's intense heat that causes the cones to begin opening. Following a burn, the cones release most of their seeds on the newly sterilized, nutrient-enriched soil where competition from other species is reduced. Such delayed seed dispersal enables a species to regenerate quickly in the aftermath of a burn.

Although not truly serotinous, the Torrey pine possesses some closed-cone traits. Mature Torrey pine cones start opening during the hot days of late summer, and gradually release some of their seeds, although a portion stays within the cones, which may remain attached to the limbs for up to 15 years. Should a tree die from drought, for example, those seeds retained by the persistent cones serve as a reservoir for following years when growing conditions might be more advantageous. If a fire and its subsequent benefits occur during a year of low cone production, having seeds available from previous years becomes an asset. The Torrey pine's protective cones with thick scales, and its big seeds capable of rapid root growth, are other indications that the species may have adapted to wildfire.

At the Reserve, the Torrey pine has clearly benefited from recent fires. Following an arsonist's blaze in 1972, many seedlings emerged within the burned area. Seven years later, the new saplings far outnumbered the old trees killed by the fire. In adjacent unburned areas no seedlings

Following a series of droughts, nearly 15 percent of the Reserve's pines were killed by bark beetles. The tiny insects can colonize a tree within hours.

were found. Similar results were obtained from several small test burns conducted during the mid-1980s.

Bark Beetles, Drought, and Pheromones

In the late 1980s, a combination of natural events devastated portions of the Reserve's most scenic groves. During the winter of 1988, fierce winds toppled several dozen trees. The freshly downed trees helped attract and nurture populations of the California five-spined ips, a native bark beetle. By the following spring, the tiny beetles had invaded the recently killed trees and were breeding in earnest. Once established, they moved to neighboring live trees and within a few years had spread throughout portions of the Reserve's drought-stressed woodlands.

Adult beetles bore through a tree's bark and deposit their eggs in the cambium layer. When hatched, beetle larvae feed on this vital tissue until they reach adulthood and repeat the cycle, which only takes four to six weeks. To assault and weaken a living tree, the beetles must attack en

By following cracks in the soft sandstone, Torrey pine roots often hasten erosion, which can lead to a tree's demise.

masse. They achieve this by emitting a sex scent, or pheromone, that attracts more beetles. As the infestation continues, reaching densities that threaten their host pine and food source, the beetles decrease production of the attractant and produce another type of pheromone that sends a repelling signal.

Under normal conditions, healthy pines can repulse the invaders with the internal pressure of their sap by "pitching them out." The infestation at Torrey Pines was unusually vigorous and coincided with a prolonged period of drought. By 1990, state park scientists began working with researchers from the University of California at Riverside and the California Department of Forestry to intervene. They were able to draw beetles away from besieged trees by employing pheromone lures placed in plastic funnel traps. In 1991, U.S. Forest Service scientists and Reserve staff installed an extensive system of these pheromone-baited traps amongst the dead trees. As an additional tactic, they placed anti-aggregation pheromone release devices in adjacent live trees to repel beetles from uninfested areas. About 15 percent of the pines were lost before these voracious insects were halted in late 1992. Without human intervention, the Reserve's entire Torrey pine population could have been destroyed.

An Invisible Threat

The greatest obstacle to the long-term survival of the Torrey pine is inherent in the species itself: the pines at the Reserve and on Santa Rosa Island have no genetic variability. Within the two populations, which are slightly different from each other, every tree may be a virtual clone of its neighbors. Possession of such a homogeneous gene pool makes the Torrey pine highly unusual among conifers, which normally display a great deal of variation between individuals of a given species. Due to this lack of genetic diversity, both populations of the Torrey pine are extremely vulnerable to disease, new strains of pests, or changes in their environment. Their capacity to adapt to environmental changes is practically nonexistent.

Lack of genetic variability within the Reserve's trees may be the result of climatic changes in the not-too-distant past. This theory holds that the Torrey pine population was severely reduced, perhaps to a mere handful of beleaguered trees, when the region was afflicted by intense drought 3,000 to 8,500 years ago. The arrival of desert flora on the coast, such as Mojave yucca and various cacti, appears to have coincided with this extremely arid period.

According to genetic theory, if the number of pines dropped below about 50, even for a few generations, genetic variation would be virtually eliminated. All succeeding offspring, no matter how plentiful, would carry nearly identical characteristics to those few original survivors. Many subsequent generations would be required for new traits to evolve and diversify the species' genetic bank. This suggests that the Torrey pine's near oblivion was recent; not enough time has elapsed for variation to be reintroduced.

The most plausible explanation for the island pines' genetic uniformity is that the population was founded from a mainland seed source, perhaps as recently as 18,000 years ago. Seeds that floated or were somehow transported to the

*W*ithin *the diverse landscape at Torrey Pines, each tree develops a unique appearance. But genetically, all the trees are identical.*

island would carry only a partial sample of the parent grove's potential gene pool, which may have already been lacking in variation. Researchers speculate that climatic fluctuations had greatly reduced the mainland populations, leading to limited genetic diversity in the surviving stands. Under this hypothesis, had the island group been founded much earlier, it is likely there would be more differences between the two current populations.

This resilient conifer reflects a long history of escaping, adapting, and enduring hostile circumstances. Now reduced to two small native populations and hampered by limited genetic resources, the Torrey pine is a species in jeopardy.

Southern California's smog often intensifies the colors of sunsets. The region's air pollution may also pose a threat to the Torrey pine, because the species bears no genetic diversity and is therefore highly vulnerable to environmental changes. Fortunately, prevailing ocean breezes tend to carry few air pollutants. The Torrey pine is also relatively tolerant of ozone, a component of smog that is deadly to some other conifers, such as ponderosa and Jeffrey pines.

*T*he relentless processes of weathering and erosion sculpt these golden bluffs of Torrey sandstone. Sediments bound up in this ancient formation are slowly released back to the sea. Over time they may be reconsolidated into a new generation of sandstone, whose destiny could be to repeat what's happening here.

33

The Torrey pine takes advantage of every apparent opportunity in order to survive. Here, a tree's roots have penetrated a crack along a cliff edge too successfully and wedged away the weak sandstone. Suspended against the vertical canyon wall, the larger, exposed roots will grow a protective covering of bark. The tiny feeder roots will dry up and fall away.

*D*aily tides and waves continually redesign the surface of the beach. These classic ripple marks are usually best seen during low tide in places where the beach's gradient is very gentle. A combination of interrelated factors must exist before the tiny dune-like forms can be created: the water must be the right depth, move at the proper velocity, and flow over sand grains of appropriate size.

Coastal agave is well equipped to live in a semi-arid environment. Its succulent, water-storing leaves are covered by a thick cuticle that reduces evaporative loss. The slightly concave leaves also help channel any precipitation toward the plant's roots. After growing slowly for a number of years, the agave commits all of its energy to producing a tall stalk topped by yellow flowers. Following this growth spurt, which may occur anytime from September to May, the plant dies.

Beginning in February, bush poppies often inaugurate the long springtime wildflower season at Torrey Pines. Their blossoms are two inches across, and the plants may grow from three to ten feet high. Bush poppies, which are part of the chaparral community, are well adapted to fire and usually flourish in years following burns. Their tiny seeds readily germinate after they have been seared by fire.

Velvet cactus is mainly restricted to the maritime bluffs of northwestern Baja California and is quite rare in San Diego County. It also grows on several islands off the southern California coast. Botanists of the U.S.-Mexican Boundary Survey first described the species in 1850, the same year that Charles Parry named the Torrey pine. Mojave yucca is more widespread and flourishes in desert and semi-arid coastal regions of California and Baja.

*R*unoff from winter storms often inundates the salt pans around Los Peñasquitos Lagoon and provides an expanded haven for numerous species of migrating water-fowl. By summer the shallow ponds are gone, replaced by a maze of cracked, sun-baked mud.

*F*lanked by the Pacific Ocean on the west and otherwise surrounded by an increasingly urban environment, Torrey Pines is a virtual wilderness island. As new development eliminates neighboring natural communities and further isolates the Reserve, the biodiversity preserved at Torrey Pines becomes more valuable. Any loss of species would be difficult to replace.

The Reserve's prominent sandstone outcroppings create a precarious foundation for numerous species of plants. Bush sunflower, buckwheat, sea dahlia, Torrey pine, coast barrel cactus, and prickly pear all vie for footing on the steep slopes. Trees whose roots are loosened become vulnerable to high winds.

*F*og benefits the vegetation of this semi-arid coast by moderating temperatures and helping plants reduce water loss by transpiration. In addition to its ecological role, fog imposes a hushed beauty upon the Reserve. Most visitors are reluctant to venture forth when dense fog settles in, and they miss the wonderful changes it produces at Torrey Pines.

At dawn, a veneer of fog often mantles the cliffs and shore. This is the hour when the timeless boundary between land and sea becomes blurred. An occasional shorebird provides the only evidence of the diverse forms of life whose primordial ancestors once paused on this ancient threshold.

More than 300 species of native plants grow at Torrey Pines.

THREE

ITSELF, ALONE, UNIMITATED

I believe there is one impression that stands out eminently above all others—that is the distinctiveness of this one spot.... It is itself, alone, unimitated.

—Ralph Cornell, 1922

A dramatic landscape greets the visitor to Torrey Pines State Reserve. Towering sea cliffs, sweeping ocean views, wind-sculpted pine groves, and breathtaking wildflower displays are among the unforgettable offerings of this coastal preserve. But there is much to discover beyond the celebrated scenery. The solitude of a quiet trail, the curling crest of a backlit wave, or the fragrance of rain-soaked chaparral equally contribute to the Reserve's overall richness. Unexpected finds, be they fragile fossils or tiny orchids, awaken the senses to this diverse environment and kindle deep admiration for the natural order. Torrey Pines is a place for walking slowly.

Exploring the Headlands

The entire Reserve abounds with beauty, but few areas of Torrey Pines are as enchanting as the headlands. Because the upland terrain is so varied, even a short walk becomes an unpredictable treasure hunt. A hiker might encounter a horned lizard dozing along a sun-warmed section of trail, spot a great horned owl roosting in a pine, or sight a California gray whale surfacing offshore.

Along hundreds of miles of coast, the Reserve is the only location that supports native pines. In some pockets, the trees are dense enough to form groves that convey the feeling of a forest community. Trails meander through these woodlands, where the air is scented by pine pitch and the wind whispers through needled boughs. Often masked by the drone of breaking waves, the unexpected sound of sighing pines is a special treat in this semi-arid setting.

Leaving the intimacy of shaded groves, paths abruptly lead to windswept bluffs high above the shore. During spring, these open slopes are often tinted yellow, purple, and white by carpets of poppies, lupines, and other

Torrey Pines is renowned for its spring wildflower display. For several months each year the sunny cliff tops are awash with color.

wildflowers. The cliff-top trails and overlooks are ideal for observing wildlife along the shoreline below. One may see sanderlings scoot across damp beach sand or watch strings of brown pelicans gliding effortlessly along the ridges of surging waves. Bottlenose dolphins sometimes torpedo toward the shore in rising swells or frolic just beyond the surf line in a clear and glassy sea.

Inland from the expansive cliff tops, trails reenter Torrey Pines' unique blend of woods and chaparral. Backslopes and side canyons are quiet, shielded from the sound of spilling waves and onshore winds. Here, the still air often comes alive with the songs and activities of the Reserve's rich assortment of birds. The melancholy call of a mourning dove may float down a draw, countered by the staccato shriek of a northern flicker. From deep in the chaparral comes the bouncing-ball call of a wrentit. Towhees busily scratch through duff and litter in the underbrush, while Nuttall's woodpeckers chisel the bark on trunks and limbs. Vocal flocks of bushtits flit from shrub to shrub in search of food.

Some of the most impressive terrain on the headlands is reminiscent of desert badlands. The sandy, poorly consolidated sediments of Torrey Pines' seaward basins are readily affected by erosion and support little vegetation. Each year, runoff from winter storms resculpts these vulnerable deposits, carving them into barren labyrinths and braided gullies. Intricately eroded palisades ring steep-walled basins and buttress precipitous ridges.

In places, the Reserve's mesa tops are sparsely vegetated and display an austere beauty. The mesas are remnants of an old marine terrace, which originally formed when waves cut a bench along an ancient and now uplifted shoreline. Parts of the terrace are nearly devoid of topsoil, its surface stripped down to an impervious sandstone crust. Although these exposed, open flats support few plants, they are home to one of California's rarest species: the dwarf dudleya. This inch-high succulent, which appears for a few months each year, is found only at Torrey Pines and three other nearby sites.

Torrey Pines' headlands also provide vantage points from which to contemplate the abundant biodiversity of the neighboring sea. Onshore, dense stands of twiggy chamise and other chaparral shrubs form an elfin forest. Bobcats, skunks, woodrats, rattlesnakes, and quail are a few of the creatures that come here to forage, hunt, and hide. Offshore, giant bladder kelp grows toward the ocean's sunlit surface in hundred-foot-high columns, forming a complex submarine forest. Jellyfish, sand dollars, and spiny lobster shells occasionally wash onto the beach and serve as intriguing reminders of the wealth of aquatic life that flourishes beyond the cliff tops.

Plants of a Desert Coast

Southern California's Pacific shore is often described as a coastal desert. Torrey Pines receives an average annual rainfall of about ten inches, only three and a half inches more than the western edge of the Colorado Desert, 55 miles inland. Despite its semi-arid Mediterranean climate—short, mild winters with little rainfall and long, dry summers—Torrey Pines supports a rich flora. More

The presence of fishhook cactus at the Reserve comes as a surprise to most visitors.

than 300 native species of plants grow within the Reserve.

With the exception of the salt marsh at Los Peñasquitos Lagoon, most of the vegetation at Torrey Pines belongs to one of two widespread and frequently overlapping plant communities: coastal sage scrub and chaparral. These two groups are dominated by different plant species, and both communities are well adapted to the modest rainfall, prolonged summer drought, and wildfires that shape their environment.

Coastal sage scrub is the more drought-adapted of the two communities and typically occupies the driest sites at Torrey Pines. Many of its key species are low-growing, woody shrubs with soft aromatic leaves, such as California sagebrush, black sage, and the rare Cleveland sage. These sages are drought-deciduous and respond to the aridity of summer by shedding their leaves. Flat-top buckwheat is also a common member of this community.

Chaparral is a taller and more complex plant community dominated by evergreen shrubs with rigid, nearly wilt-proof leaves. The most widespread chaparral plant of Torrey Pines is chamise, a species which often forms impenetrable stands on the mesas. In moist areas and on north-facing slopes, chamise grows in association with coast scrub oak, lemonade berry, toyon, manzanita, and ceanothus.

In order to contend with summer conditions, chaparral species have developed a variety of leaf types. Toyon, coast scrub oak, and most other evergreens have leaves that minimize evaporative loss with a thick waxy coating on their surfaces. Laurel sumac leaves fold along the midline to reduce exposure to the sun. Yerba santa leaves are covered by a fine light fuzz that deflects harsh sunlight and helps keep them cool; in times of drought, they drop off the plant.

Perhaps the most indicative plants of the desert coast are the agave, yuccas, and cacti of Torrey Pines. Some of these species may have always grown in this semi-arid climate, while others are probably holdovers from a period that followed the Ice Age when the regional climate became very dry and desert species migrated from inland areas to the coast. Among the most conspicuous plants at Torrey Pines is Mojave yucca, a well-known species of the Mojave and Colorado deserts. Armed with bayonet-like leaves and crowned each season by a showy mass of cream-colored flowers, the yucca strikes an impressive, if incongruous, pose against an ocean backdrop. The Reserve is also a northern mainland outpost for coastal agave and velvet cactus, prominent members of the succulent-sage scrub of coastal northwestern Baja California. Torrey Pines is one of the few places north of the Mexican border where these plants grow in the wild.

The Reserve is also home to several other species of cactus. Two types of cholla, or "jumping cactus," grow here: coast cholla, which is multi-branched and erect, and snake cholla, which sprawls on the ground. Coast prickly pear, with its green pads, yellow blossoms, and large red fruit also prospers in the Reserve. Coast barrel cactus thrives in a variety of seemingly marginal locations at Torrey Pines. One can even find the diminutive fishhook cactus.

One of Torrey Pines' more uncommon plants is the rein orchid, a species which seems out of place along this semi-arid coast. Unlike its moisture-loving relatives, this small orchid often grows in exposed, dry sites. Its pale green, fragrant flowers appear in spring and measure a half-inch across; they adorn single spikes a few feet tall. The slender shafts are hard to spot, but once found and closely inspected, they reveal the miniature gem-like blossoms.

Torrey Pines offers a refreshing contrast to the surrounding urban environment, which has been transformed by imported water and exotic vegetation. The pine is understandably the most famous plant of the Reserve, but the rest of the native flora preserved here would warrant special attention even if the trees were absent. This landscape is a last, undeveloped vestige of southern California's desert coast.

Cliffs, Cobbles, and Ancient Rivers

Visitors who stroll along Torrey Pines State Beach are treated to a different perspective of the Reserve. In viewing the towering sea bluffs from the shore, one can contemplate the geologic processes of deposition, uplift, and erosion that have produced the Reserve's foundation.

Most of Torrey Pines' geologic story is recorded in the exposed rock of the cliff faces. The topographic bulk that forms the northern headlands began as a sequence of marine sediments deposited 45 to 50 million years ago. The greenish lower half of the cliffs consists of shales and siltstones that are rich in fossil oysters and other sea shells. These fine-grained sediments and their marine fossils indicate deposition in calm shallow bays and estuaries. The upper cliffs comprise multiple layers of nearly pure sandstone. Cross-bedding in these deposits suggests they also accumulated in shallow waters, but where tidal currents were stronger along the inland edges of barrier islands in the coastal sea. Geologists point out that these two formations were deposited at roughly the same time. During a complex sequence of fluctuating sea levels and changes in the level of the land, the shoreline migrated back and forth. When sea level rose, for example, the shore moved inland and sand from the coastal deposits was driven by waves over the adjacent silt-rich lagoons.

Capping the bluffs are remnants of more recent shore deposits. These formed within the last million years at a time when the land was again undergoing intermittent uplift and the ocean level was fluctuating. During pauses in the uplift, broad platforms known as wave-cut benches were carved into the coast by advancing waves. Torrey Pines' rust-colored sandstone mesa is the most conspicuous and one of the oldest of the Reserve's marine terraces. As recently as 120,000 years ago, waves cut another bench in the bottom of the Reserve's seaward-facing basins. A thin layer of seashells, visible in sections of cliff about 50 feet above the beach, reveals its location.

The beach seems to change little from day to day, but on an annual basis waves rearrange the loose sediment along the shore. With the arrival of winter, powerful storm waves strip the beach of its mantle of sand and pull it offshore, uncovering beds of smooth, fine-textured cobbles. Seeming out of place along a coast formed from sedimentary rocks, the hard stones lie exposed until gentler summer waves restore the sand and bury them again. The cobbles remain interred until Pacific storms return in late fall and the cycle begins anew.

The cobbles that are piled on the beach or found in the headlands were not produced at Torrey Pines. Revealing a long life of abrasion, they arrived at the ocean's edge

---

Old sandstones at the cliff's base resist erosion more than the much younger sediments above.

via fast-flowing rivers that deposited them on floodplains and deltas over millions of years. The durable stones have been reworked and moved many times by subsequent cycles of erosion and redistribution, both by streams and by waves.

The ancient rivers are long gone, but geologists have identified some of the areas from which the cobbles probably derived. Most of the water-worn stones correspond to metavolcanic rocks in southern California's Santa Ana Mountains. Others appear to have come from much farther afield. They match 150 million-year-old volcanic bedrock found in Sonora, Mexico, 270 miles to the southeast. These cobbles were carried westward by rivers 40 to 50 million years ago and deposited as massive conglomerates along the coast. Horizontal displacements along the continental margin later rafted the Sonoran coast northwest to the San Diego region where the cobbles were redistributed by further erosion. These old cobbles may have been

transported as far by movement of tectonic plates as by the rivers that first tumbled them to the sea.

The Quiet Wetlands

The largest and least visited area of Torrey Pines is Los Peñasquitos Lagoon. With its carpets of pickleweed, glistening mudflats, and turbid waters, the lagoon looks barren and lifeless. In fact, however, the salt marsh and its associated wetlands comprise the Reserve's most fertile and dynamic ecosystem.

The site of today's lagoon was once a deep-cut river valley. The most recent rise in sea level, which occurred within the past 10,000 years, drowned the mouth of the valley. Over time, the embayment filled with sediments, and thus broadened, evolved into the current salt marsh.

Within the lagoon, water levels and salinity change by the hour and with the season. Rising tides introduce varying volumes of seawater, which in turn are diluted by varying quantities of freshwater from Los Peñasquitos Creek and several ephemeral streams. Most salt marsh plants must contend with swift and constant changes in their environment. During high tide they may be completely submerged, while at low tide they may be exposed to direct sunlight and drying winds.

Lagoon plants face their greatest challenge in coping with excess salt. They must prevent its intake or dispose of surplus amounts that build up within their cells. Some species, such as pickleweed and California seablite, dilute the salt with water stored in their cells; the extra fluid gives them a fleshy, succulent appearance. Salt grass, sea lavender, and alkali heath are able to excrete excess salt directly through special pores. Low levels of oxygen in the lagoon's

The Belding's savannah sparrow, an endangered species, nests in pickleweed at Los Peñasquitos Lagoon.

ITSELF, ALONE, UNIMITATED

waterlogged soil present another obstacle to plant growth. Several species overcome this by developing air spaces within their roots to facilitate oxygen storage.

The wetlands support a diverse fauna. Clams, mussels, worms, and snails dwell in the nutrient-rich mud. Ghost shrimp and numerous kinds of crabs scavenge the murky depths. At least 15 species of fish inhabit the meandering channels, including California halibut, which use the lagoon's shallow waters as a nursery before venturing to sea.

Various mammals also depend on the marshlands. Rabbits, mice, and ornate shrews forage amidst the surrounding grasslands. Ground squirrels and pocket gophers burrow along neighboring embankments. Tracks in the mud confirm the nocturnal forays of raccoons, weasels, and coyotes. Trails of heart-shaped imprints record the silent passage of mule deer.

Many of the Reserve's over 200 bird species can be observed in the vicinity of the wetlands. Los Peñasquitos Lagoon is a critical stopover point for legions of birds that migrate along the Pacific Flyway. As one of southern California's last coastal salt marshes, it is an especially important sanctuary for dozens of species that seek out its protected wetlands for resting, feeding, and nesting.

At low tide, the lagoon's exposed sediments become a banquet table for deep-probing shorebirds. Godwits, avocets, and black-necked stilts patrol the waterways, plunging their long bills deep into the mud in search of worms and clams. Waders such as great blue herons and snowy egrets stalk the shallow back channels, snatching

A variety of fish and many invertebrate species thrive in the placid waters of Los Peñasquitos Lagoon.

small fish with lightning jabs of their spear-like bills.

Depending on the season, a variety of ducks and other waterfowl drift about the quiet lagoon. Grebes, loons, and cormorants dive for fish, while mallards and teal descend for mollusks and bottom vegetation. Terns, kingfishers, and an occasional osprey plummet from the sky to catch fish. Keen-eyed raptors silently circle overhead in search of insects, rodents, and smaller birds. Cattail thickets near the lagoon's freshwater inlets host red-winged blackbirds, marsh wrens, and yellowthroats. Belding's savannah sparrows—now among California's rarest songbirds—nest in the pickleweed matting.

Fog, the Agile Performer

One of the best times to experience Torrey Pines is when it is engulfed by dense fog. As it creeps on-shore, coastal fog becomes an integral part of the landscape and dramatically alters the Reserve's character. Along the beach, notions of time and space dissolve in the graying light as familiar landmarks quietly disappear. At times, even the edge of the sea is invisible, and the looming cliffs are detected only by intuition. If the ocean is calm and the fog lies still, the unsuspecting beach walker may be startled by a sea lion's coarse bark or the phantom movement of a shorebird.

Dense fog temporarily converts the semi-arid Reserve into a landscape of damp silhouettes.

An equally eerie experience awaits the visitor over-taken by fog while hiking a cliff-top trail or pausing at an ocean overlook. The normally majestic views of the coast and Pacific horizon are quickly consumed by the incoming fog. Unable to peer beyond or below a fog-bound precipice, one feels poised at land's end, as the dash of distant surf and the smell of salt spray drift up through the fathomless haze.

Thick fog becomes an agile performer in the Reserve's steep-walled canyons. Prodded by the wind, it scales the cliffs, pours through the gaps, and floats up the arroyos. In the deep ravines, dense pockets of fog coalesce and dissipate in quick succession, alternately obscuring and revealing the surrounding terrain.

Among the pines and chaparral, fog imposes a magical order. Each grove and shrub-covered slope becomes a mute symphony of colorless shapes and silhou-ettes. Tiny beads of moisture collect on the fragile strands of spiders' webs, delicately tracing their outlines. Damp air coaxes rich woodland scents from the trees. The muffled patter from dripping pine needles is the only sound that emanates from the hushed landscape. Wrapped in the silence and shadowless light of a foggy day, the relict pines seem even more mysterious.

Traces of the Past

In scattered openings throughout the chapar-ral lie accumulations of broken cobbles, stone fragments, and sharp flakes. The hard-edged stones are conspicuous among the upland's predominantly smooth, rounded rocks. These stones were not chipped or fractured by natural forces, but altered by human hands. They are man-made artifacts, tangible traces of prehistoric people who lived here for generations. Dark-soiled kitchen middens and piles of bleached shells are other signs that attest to a long history of human presence at Torrey Pines.

Several different cultural groups have lived in and around Torrey Pines. The first group of humans, referred to as the San Dieguito Culture, came to the area about 11,000 years ago. These nomadic hunters located their camps inland from the coastal strip but traveled to seaside lagoons and wetlands to hunt and fish.

About 7,500 years ago a new group became the dominant culture; anthropologists refer to them as the La Jollans. They settled along the immediate coast, including Torrey Pines, and inhabited the region for nearly 6,000 years. The La Jollans were replaced by the Diegueño, or Kumeyaay, approximately 1,500 years ago. They were present when Europeans arrived, and their descendants still reside in San Diego County.

The majority of archaeological sites within the Reserve are associated with the La Jollans. They left rather crude implements, reflecting a culture primarily sustained by gathering rather than hunting. Whole cobbles were used for milling and grinding, while others were hammered apart to make tools for cutting and chopping. Some of the broken rocks were cracked by the heat of cook fires, while others, concentrated in charcoal-rich soil, may indicate the location of ancient sweat lodges. Unlike the San Dieguito or Kumeyaay cultures, the La Jollans left no finely crafted spear points or arrowheads. Even rudimentary projectile points are rare. The La Jollans relied on plants, seeds, and abundant shellfish, which they supplemented with fish and small game.

The fire-darkened stones and primitive tools stimulate our curiosity about who their vanished makers were and how they lived. While thumbing the ragged edge of a scraper or hefting a discarded hammerstone, we may well wonder about our own place in history.

Rhythms of the Land

Few urban preserves are as accessible and ecologically diverse as Torrey Pines. Within minutes of arriving at the Reserve, one can become immersed in its natural terrain. From wooded glens to boggy mudflats, there is always something to observe, ponder, and appreciate.

Like all natural environments, Torrey Pines exhibits rhythms and cycles. Each day and season chronicles the habitual momentum of life, whether evidenced by fresh tracks along game paths or marked by the return of migrating monarch butterflies on a brilliant fall morning. Throughout the year the Reserve's abundant flora changes like a color-coded calendar as something comes into bloom each month. Grunion time their spring and summer beach spawns to particular high tides and specific waves. The crack of pine cones popping open during the hot, dry days of early autumn announces the turn of another cycle.

The observant visitor greets each change as an expected old friend. One excitedly anticipates the bloom of a cherished flower, the arrival of a favorite bird, or the winter day when an extra-low tide briefly exposes a hidden reef.

This preserve is far more than a wilderness enclave for rare trees. Torrey Pines is also a sanctuary for rejuvenating the human spirit. Through its diversity, it fosters love and respect for the natural world. For that, it is a priceless treasure.

*V*isitors are drawn to Torrey Pines for many reasons. Some seek the solace of a wooded path. Others come to view wildflowers or look for birds around Los Peñasquitos Lagoon. For others, watching waves splash against the base of the cliff is ample reward.

Clouds from a clearing rainstorm are a welcome site at Torrey Pines. Flora at the Reserve must survive on an average of only ten inches of precipitation each year, most of which falls during the winter months. During drought years, the pines become extremely vulnerable to various boring insects.

Following a long period of drought, this 200-year-old tree was killed by bark beetles. Most of the adjacent pines suffered the same fate. As part of a reforestation project, scientists and Reserve managers collected cones from the dead trees, germinated their seeds, and raised seedlings that were planted in the same areas where the parent trees once grew.

Torrey sandstone weathers into a rugged complex of chutes and hollows. Along the western edge of the headlands this 45-million-year-old formation is topped by darker shore deposits that are less than 120,000 years old. The contact between these two formations represents a huge gap in the Reserve's geologic record.

*L*os Peñasquitos Lagoon is a complex, fertile habitat that supports a mixture of plants and animals adapted to the part aquatic, part terrestrial salt marsh. Only the hardiest and most resourceful species can live in this environment where the degree of salinity and level of water can change by the hour. For thousands of years Native Americans camped nearby to harvest the lagoon's abundant shellfish.

Cliff-top Torrey pines near the ocean often grow little more than a few inches each year. Onshore winds and salty air tend to draw moisture from the pines, which can cause exposed parts of a tree's crown to die back. Torrey pines do not produce new lateral shoots to replace the tips of damaged branches that have been pruned by the elements.

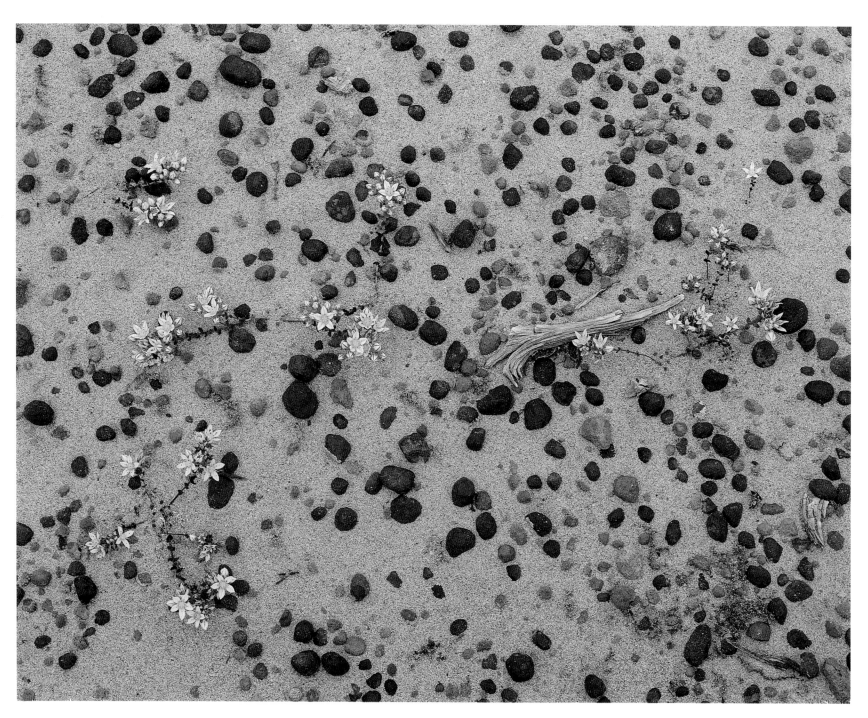

Short-leaved, or dwarf, dudleya is extremely rare and occurs only at the Reserve and three other nearby sites. In spring these tiny succulents emerge from an underground stem and produce small dark buttons that closely resemble the pebble-like stones among which they grow. After blooming, the above-ground parts whither away and nothing remains to reveal the plants' presence until new growth appears the following spring.

Two species of verbena are found at Torrey Pines. Beach sand verbena (shown here) generally occurs along the tops of seaward bluffs. It grows on sunny, south- or west-facing slopes in loose sandy soil. Beach sand verbena often blooms all year long and during the dry summer months offers a cheery spot of color.

Chinese houses, California poppies, and cream cups are but a few of the species that grow on the north-facing slopes that border Los Peñasquitos Lagoon. Although the Reserve is only about 1,750 acres in size, one fifth of all the native plant species in San Diego County are found here. This number is especially impressive in light of the fact that the county comprises coastal, mountain, and desert regions.

*T*orrey pine roots are most likely to become exposed on steep canyon walls where the sandstone is easily eroded. These narrow canyons remain shady and cool until late spring and they retain moisture longer than other areas of the Reserve. California polypody, one of eight species of ferns found at Torrey Pines, thrives in these damp canyon grottos just a short distance from sun-baked chaparral on the mesa tops.

It is difficult to define the allure of the Torrey pine. Other pine species grow bigger, live longer, and are even rarer. In its native habitat, the Torrey pine subsists in poor, sandy soil, survives on meager rainfall, and is often subject to constant wind and salt spray. Our interest in the tree may be as simple as an appreciation for a tenacious species that exhibits an affinity for a challenging environment.

*O*vercast, gloomy days some-times produce the most interesting natural light. The clouds of a slow-moving winter storm cast a chilling hue as they amass along the coast. The subdued light enhances the primitive beauty of land, sea, and sky. Cobbles seem to mysteriously emerge from the sand as powerful waves alter the beach for another season.

The eroded sea bluffs are a major attraction for many visitors at Torrey Pines.

FOUR

WHOSE HERITAGE IT IS

Torrey Pines…can be likened to a museum that contains objects of priceless worth for it offers sanctuary and protection of these struggling survivors of a past age. But the sanctity of this refuge can only be preserved insofar as the people, whose heritage it is, zealously guard and maintain it in its primitive beauty.

—Guy L. Fleming, 1942

S an Diegans took a visionary stand in 1899 when they established a "free and public park" as a means of safeguarding the Torrey pine. Yet despite a century of expanding protection at the Reserve, the tree and the landscape it inhabits face a variety of challenges. It has become clear that ensuring the ecological well-being of Torrey Pines State Reserve is a complex responsibility. Much remains to be learned about managing this precious remnant of our natural heritage.

In the Absence of Fire

Modern studies have shown that setting aside and protecting habitats is a beginning, but not an end, in the battle to conserve ecosystems and rare species. In nature, nothing is so constant as change; as a result, preservation efforts aimed at maintaining the status quo of a natural area often fail. At the Reserve, for example, decades of fire suppression have probably hindered pine regeneration and created a population in which old trees far outnumber saplings. Without occasional wildfires, the groves' dense undergrowth and organic litter build up, which prevents pine seeds from reaching bare soil and germinating. Although test burns have increased the number of Torrey pine seedlings, the introduction of fire around living trees is controversial; controlled burns carry the risk of killing mature pines.

In contrast to the Reserve, the number of young Torrey pines on Santa Rosa Island has dramatically increased within the past 100 years. However, sample cores from the island pines have revealed that they were rarely exposed to fire during that time. This population's high rate of regeneration may be attributed to a different form of disturbance: grazing by sheep and cattle. Sheep were introduced to the island in the 1880s and were later replaced by cattle early in the twentieth century. Ecologists for the National Park Service, which now administers Santa Rosa Island, surmise that grazing has served as something of a substitute for fire. The cattle control competitive grasses and herbs while leaving pine seedlings uneaten. Within the next 20 years the island's livestock will be removed and in their absence the groves' native understory is expected to become reestablished. When this transition is complete, some researchers believe the pines' reproduction rate may gradually decrease.

The viability of the Reserve's natural communities is threatened by encroaching urbanization.

Plans to encourage Torrey pine regeneration with fire have been postponed until further studies are completed.

A number of other species in the Reserve's chaparral and coastal sage scrub communities are also revitalized by fire. Many annual wildflowers flourish following a burn and are often the first of a whole succession of plants that respond favorably to episodes of fire. In the prolonged absence of fire, some species might disappear altogether. Resource ecologists are now evaluating the use of prescribed burns for managing the chaparral and maintaining the Reserve's rich floral diversity.

Multiply and Divide

Although the entire Reserve is managed to maintain the health of its ecosystems, the Torrey pine receives special attention because of its rarity and genetic limitations. The primary strategy for perpetuating the species has been to maximize its numbers within its native habitat. The "warehousing" of Torrey pine specimens and seeds in various botanic gardens and herbariums provides added insurance against catastrophic loss should the natural populations disappear.

A problem facing resource managers is the lack of information about the ideal structure of Torrey pine populations. Some foresters feel that the Reserve's current number of trees is artificially high, perhaps as a result of tree planting earlier this century. Regeneration efforts have been designed to determine the best conditions for seedling establishment as well as the optimal density for the pines. Reforestation based simply on "more is better" may not be appropriate. If the trees became too numerous they would compete for limited water resources, especially during droughts. This could lead to stressed stands that are vulnerable to beetle infestations. If the pines are too closely packed, bark beetles could more quickly move from one tree to another.

The Torrey pine rarely naturalizes outside of its native habitat, but a well-documented exception is taking place at La Purísima Mission State Historical Park on the central California coast northwest of Santa Barbara. Here Torrey pines are thriving in what may be part of their historic range. Planted during reconstruction of the mission in the 1930s by the California Conservation Corps, they have successfully reproduced and spread to the surrounding hills. This natural propagation, however, is viewed as detrimental by some ecologists. They believe that the pines compete with species in the local chaparral community. Others regard the pines as nonnatives that should be removed to help preserve the historic flavor of La Purísima's early mission days.

Natural Communities at Risk

At the Reserve, the rare conifer is not the only species at risk. Adverse influences generated by the growth of San Diego, currently the nation's sixth largest city, are mounting. Urban landscaping is a source of invasive exotic plants, some of which can easily out-compete the Reserve's indigenous species. Of Torrey Pines' nearly

Goldenbush and deerweed must compete with non-native iceplant at Los Peñasquitos Lagoon.

400 plant species, one quarter are nonnative. Many botanists fear that, if left unchecked, the exotics could gradually transform the Reserve's distinctive plant communities. Accordingly, the removal of such imports as pampas grass, Russian thistle, and iceplant is an ongoing project, dependent on community volunteers. Encroaching roads and development raise concerns because they interrupt wildlife

Great-horned owls nest on the Reserve's steep canyon walls and depend on its open spaces for hunting.

corridors that link the Reserve with remaining pockets of nearby open space. This urbanization limits the range for fauna, especially larger mammals that require extensive territory for feeding, hunting, and breeding.

One of the Reserve's most sensitive habitats, Los Peñasquitos Lagoon, is subject to a different array of problems. Upstream grading and the permanent alteration of the lagoon's 60,000-acre watershed have caused excessive siltation during winter runoff. Highway and railway roadbeds that were built across the wetlands hinder normal tidal flushing of the salt marsh; they also restrict the lagoon's outlet to a fixed narrow channel, which is seasonally blocked by drifting beach sand. Lacking ample runoff or high tides with strong surf, this vital link to the ocean has been reopened with heavy earth-moving equipment. Municipal sewer lines adjacent to the lagoon have frequently spilled and contaminated the salt marsh.

Dilemmas arise in balancing public access to Torrey Pines against the need to protect its fragile features. As the San Diego metropolitan area grows, more and more people are drawn to the Reserve for recreation. However, not everyone is respectful of this vulnerable environment. Some visitors trample across the landscape in pursuit of shortcuts to the beach while others pick wildflowers, collect pine cones, or spread litter. A popular canyon trail was closed because hikers repeatedly carved graffiti into its sandstone walls. Mountain bikes had to be banned from the Reserve after riders caused extensive damage both on and off trails. Off-road vehicles occasionally tear up mudflats and salt pans bordering the wetlands. The cook fires of transients who camp out illegally in the Reserve's dense chaparral are potential threats. Enforcing regulations that establish the fine line between use and abuse is one of the many tasks charged to Reserve rangers.

Fortunately, many of the challenges facing the Reserve are closely monitored by the California Department of Parks and Recreation, the Torrey Pines Association, and various conservation organizations. In addition to the dedicated rangers who administer Torrey Pines, carefully trained members of the Torrey Pines Docent Society, believed to be the oldest docent society associated with a California State Park unit, staff the visitor center. These enthusiastic volunteers also lead interpretive walks and help educate the public about the Reserve's special character. Each year hundreds of school groups visit the Reserve. Numerous academic institutions conduct studies, workshops, and classes in natural history.

Surveys show that old Torrey pines now outnumber young trees. Successful replacement of the aging population with new seedlings may well depend on current research and management policies.

A Deserving Relict

In 1883 Charles Parry expressed the hope that "wiser generations" would one day be thankful that he and his contemporaries saved the Torrey pine. Parry's desire is being realized: tens of thousands of visitors come to the Reserve each year to view the enigmatic trees and enjoy their magnificent setting.

By moving to protect the Torrey pine and its habitat, we assumed an irrevocable responsibility for the species' continued existence. Certainly this tenacious relict, rare and unique among the world's flora, deserves our continued care and stewardship.

The densest fogs at Torrey Pines often form in the immediate aftermath of Santa Ana winds. High pressure centered over the Great Basin generates these hot, dry winds that blow offshore. When the pressure weakens, the heated air, having picked up moisture over the ocean, flows back towards land. It cools and condenses as it passes over the cold coastal waters and arrives as fog.

It is unusual to see waves completely inundate the beach and crash against the base of the sea cliffs. This event is most likely to occur during winter, when heavy storm swells coincide with the year's highest tides. These waves help keep the cliffs steep.

At the Reserve, the Torrey pine grows almost exclusively in Torrey sandstone. This formation is composed of sediments deposited about 45 million years ago. Around that same time, ancestors of the Torrey pine began evolving in west-central Mexico. Their modern descendants arrived at the Reserve site sometime within the last several hundred thousand years.

The coast cholla is one of two types of cholla cactus found at Torrey Pines. Cholla's spiny segments easily detach from the main stems and often take root where they fall on the ground. The California poppy is the state wildflower and generally grows in grassy regions below 2,000 feet. Poppies fold up their petals at night as well as on foggy or overcast days.

These rust-colored deposits of sandstone originated as coastal dunes blown inland from the beach around 350,000 years ago. Now the colorful sediments are found some 300 feet above the current shore, primarily due to uplift of the land.

Throughout fall and winter, the stalks and seedheads of drying grasses conceal resident beds of succulent glasswort in the uppermost sections of Los Peñasquitos Lagoon. These areas are routinely flooded by freshwater runoff during winter storms but are inundated by saltwater only during very high tides. Some 30 species of plants live within the lagoon's different tidal zones.

The variety of colors and textural patterns displayed by these wet cobbles reflects their varied origins. Most of these metavolcanic rocks came from mountains in southern California, but a few can be traced to an area in northwestern Mexico. The stones were first rounded by rivers that dragged them to the coast. Wave action continues to smooth and polish these enduring cobbles.

A small section of the Reserve's sea cliff reveals much about coastal conditions that once existed here. These mud and sand sediments accumulated in a lagoon environment characterized by shifting currents, beaches, and bars. The sloping cross beds within the layers record the different directions of the currents that deposited them.

*T*orrey pine needles normally stay on a tree for three years before dying. At the end of summer, the pines usually shed their oldest needles first, which are found closest to the tree trunk on each branch. Western dichondra, an uncommon native coastal ground-cover, grows beneath these fallen needles.

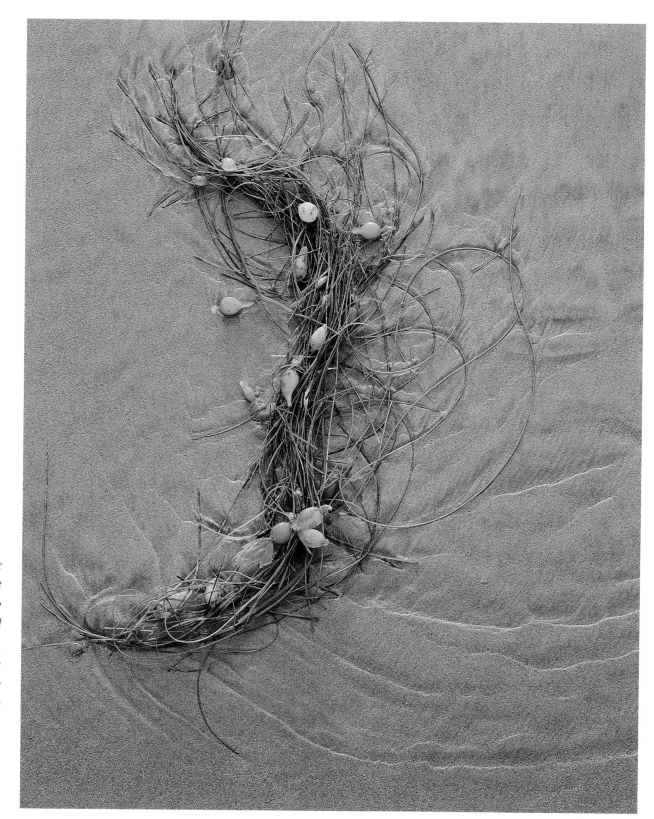

*A*lthough Torrey Pines State Beach is renowned for its ancient sea cliffs, one can also find beauty in the shoreline's ephemeral combinations of sunlight, sand, and seaweed. Bladder kelp pods and surf grass strands hint at the complex web of life that lies just beyond the beach.

Torrey pines that grow in exposed locations closest to the ocean are most vulnerable to the desiccating effects of wind and salt spray. When weakened by the added stress of droughts, such trees are usually the first to succumb to bark beetles. Dead pines do not remain standing for long, and their soft, coarse-grained wood quickly decomposes.

82

Beach primrose and sand verbena dominate a sandy rise at the southwest corner of Los Peñasquitos Lagoon. This mound is thought to be a relic sand dune, a remnant of a once widespread coastal dune system. This is the only place at Torrey Pines where two uncommon southern California species, beach lotus and golden aster, are found. Coast cholla and coast prickly pear also grow in the loose sand.

The Reserve's cliff-top trails offer a place for contemplation and unobstructed ocean views.

AFTERWORD

In 1926 Guy Fleming moved into the new caretaker's residence at Torrey Pines. This provided the Fleming and Shelton children, already well-acquainted through common interests and family ties, with ample opportunity to enjoy the "park." We delighted in exploring its sandy cliffs and ravines in their sometimes labyrinthine intricacy. There were always new places to clamber up or slide down, always inviting mats of fragrant brown needles where we could lie, looking up through the pine branches to blue sky. Sometimes we could hear the gentle swish of distant waves on the beach and wondered how best to get down there.

Such carefree frolics are now happy memories. However, the ensuing decades have nurtured another level of appreciation, one of fascination with challenges stemming from new knowledge. For example, in broader perspective, it is apparent that throughout the Southwest we are accustomed to finding pine trees in mountains or on high plateaus. Why, then, is there a compact stand of Torrey pines located close to sea level, in the southern part of the state, where the surrounding vegetation is semi-arid chaparral? And why is this patch so small? Healthy Torrey pines are common in yards and along streets of San Diego and its surroundings. Seeds and seedlings have been successfully planted in many parts of the world. If they can so easily be propagated by humans, why have they not spread farther naturally? Does the answer lie in some aspect of the location, or in the history of the trees themselves? Without a fossil record we seem to be looking at the last few sentences of a long story whose earlier chapters are still hidden from us.

Such musings make us aware that Bill Evarts has made a major contribution by opening our eyes to both the known and the unknown at Torrey Pines while at the same time treating us to a superb visual feast. Never before has so much of the essence of Torrey Pines been captured between the covers of a single volume. We come away realizing that, by force of circumstances, we are custodians of one of the rarest remnants of natural open space in the world. And that, unlike Yosemite or the Grand Canyon whose principal assets are carved in enduring stone, Torrey Pines is fragile within and vulnerable from without. The implications are clear.

—John S. Shelton

This aerial view of Torrey Pines shows the Reserve as viewed from the northwest. Photo by John S. Shelton.

PUBLISHER'S ACKNOWLEDGMENTS

The Torrey Pines Association was founded in 1950 to encourage public interest in, and support for, the preservation of the rare Torrey pine trees and their scenic refuge. This is accomplished primarily by raising funds for special projects and by publishing informative material concerning Torrey Pines State Reserve.

In the production of this book we are especially indebted to the Ellen Browning Scripps Foundation, whose generous support was a major factor in moving *Torrey Pines: Landscape and Legacy* from a dream to reality. In addition, we thank Ellen Revelle Eckis and Rollin P. Eckis for their thoughtful assistance as the book neared completion.

Among the many others whose diverse contributions helped to make the book possible, the following are also gratefully acknowledged:

Frances M. Armstrong, George and Connie Beardsley, Jack S. Bradshaw, Victoria A. Bradshaw, Barbara (Mrs. John) Cole, John Evarts, Eve Ewing, John R. Fleming, Bill and Luisa Garth, Marc Gittelsohn, David Goldberg, Nobie Hopper-Turrell, Margaret L. Langsdorf, Althea D. Lucic, Peter C. Lucic, Hamilton and Peg Marston, Don McQuiston, Harle and Ken Montgomery, Elizabeth Nicoloff, Freda M. H. Reid, Beverley Whitaker Rodgers, Catherine M. Rose, John and Mary Ann Shelton, Bruce Shetler, Sarah W. Spiess, Theodor G. Tanalski, David and Donna Weston, Thomas W. Whitaker, Robert Wohl